I LIKE TO READ
GRADE 1 READER

© 2021 Seton Press
All rights reserved.
Printed in the United States of America

Seton Press
1350 Progress Drive
Front Royal, VA 22630
Phone: (540) 636-9990
Fax: (540) 636-1602

ISBN: 978-1-60704-180-1

Illustrated by Nathan Puray

For more information, visit us on the web at
www.setonpress.com

TABLE OF CONTENTS

I Can 1

Fun 10

The Seal 19

The Hike 28

Go 39

You See, I See 48

A Rose 57

New Word List 66

I CAN

I can run.

Nat can run up the hill.

I can hop.

Pat can hop to ten.

I can sit.

Katt can sit on a box.

I can win.

Jill can win a cat.

The End

FUN

It is fun to run.

It is fun to run in a maze.

It is fun to hop.

It is fun to hop in the rain.

It is fun to wade in the lake.

It is fun to make a wave in the lake.

It is fun to sail in the bay.

It is fun to sit in the hay.

The End

THE SEAL

A seal is in the sea.

Nan and Kate see the seal.

The seal is sad.

Can we feed the seal?

Pete can feed the seal.

The seal can
eat a meal.

I can wave
to the seal.

The seal can wave to me.

The End

THE HIKE

Mike and Ava like to hike.

Mike and Ava take a kite.

Mike can tie a tail on the kite.

Mike and Ava like the kite. It is fun!

Ava can see two mice.

The mice run and hide in a pipe.

Mike can see a vine on the pipe.

Mike can see the kite tail in the vine.

Ava can see a bee hive in the vine.

It is time to end the hike!

The End

GO

We will go in a boat.

He will go on a goat.

He will go in a hole.

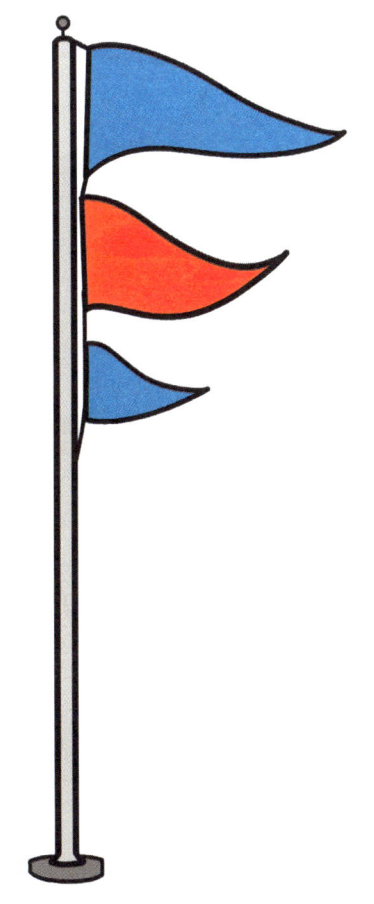

We will go
to the pole.

We will go
to the road.

He will go
see the toad.

He will go home for a bone.

I will go home
for a cone.

The End

YOU SEE, I SEE

You see a cub.

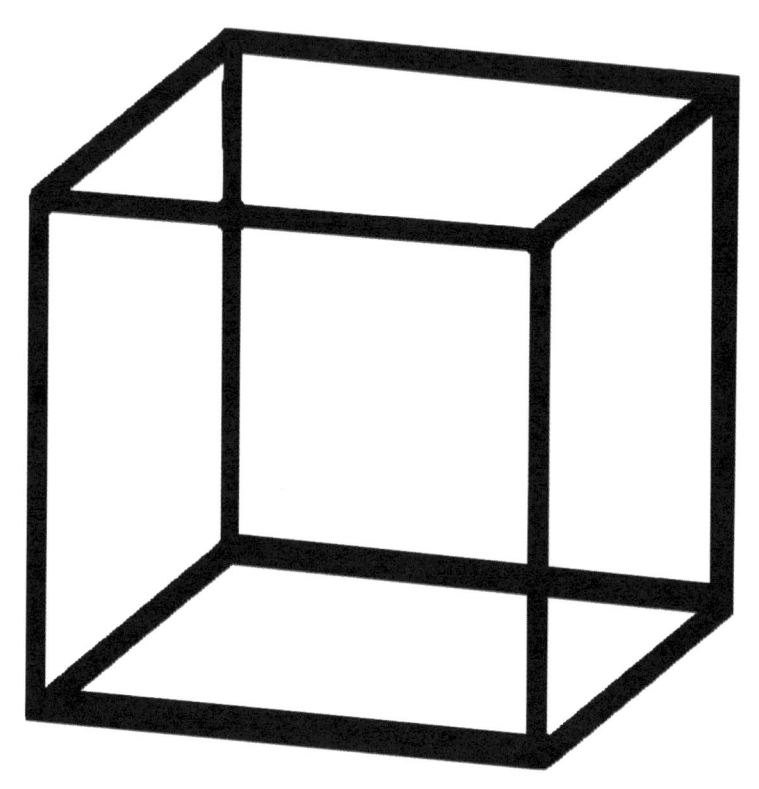

I see a cube.

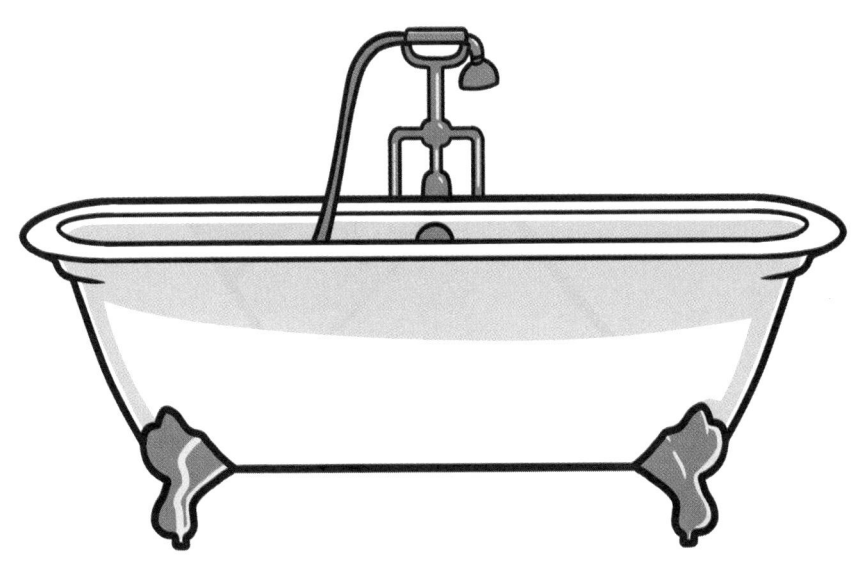

You see a tub.

I see a tube.

Did you get the lute?

No, I got the suit.

Can you see Sue?

No, I can see you.

The End

A ROSE

It is a day in May.

Dad and Mom say, "Time to go."

We are all here.

We go in the van.

We walk in.

We give a rose.

See the red rose.

It is time to go home.

The End

NEW WORD LIST

I Like to Read
I
like
to
read

I Can
a
box
can
cat
hill
hop
Jill
Katt
Nat
on
Pat

run
sit
ten
the
up
win
The End

Fun
bay
fun
hay
in
is
it
lake
make
maze

rain
sail
wade
wave

The Seal
eat
feed
Kate
me
meal
Nan
Pete
sad
sea
see
seal
we

The Hike
and
Ava
bee
hide
hike
hive
kite
mice
Mike
pipe
tail
take
tie
time
two
vine

Go
boat
bone
cone

go
goat
he
hole
home
pole
road
toad
will

You See, I See
cub
cube
did
get
got
lute
no
Sue
suit
tub

tube
you

A Rose
all
are
Dad
day
give
here
May
Mom
red
rose
say
van
walk